MINNESOTA FATS

Never Behind the Eight Ball

Fred Walter

MINNESOTA FATS

Never Behind the Eight Ball

Fred Walther

COOL
SPRINGS
PRESS

Dedicated to the memory of Rudolf Wanderone "Minnesota Fats."
He lived the life of a hustler. He took from the rich and gave to the
poor. He loved children and cared for countless animals. He did
more for pool that any other person. He became an American icon.

--F. W.

Library of Congress Cataloging-in-Publication Data

Walther, Fred, 1945 -
    Minnesota Fats : never behind the eight ball / by Fred
Walther.
        p.   cm.

        ISBN 1-888608-54-4 (pbk.)

        1. Minnesota Fats, 1913- 1996. 2. Billiard players – United
        States –
        Biography.   3. Billiards.   I. Title.

        GV892.2.M55W35   1998
        794.7'3'092 – dc21
        [B]   98-19528
                                                     CIP

Cool Springs Press, Inc.
206 Bridge Street
Franklin, TN 37064

First Printing 1998
Printed in the United States of America
10 9 8 7 6 5 4 3 2 1

Certain information included herein was published in 1966 by World
Publishing, Cleveland, in *Bank Shots and Other Great Robberies* by
Minnesota Fats with Tom Fox, and is now used with permission.

Contents

Preface   7

Introduction   11

Lessons From the Master: Minnesota   45
   Fats on Life, Love, and the Game
   of Billiards

A Few Tips, Please   101

The Master in His Element: 145
   Minnesota Fats on Eight Ball

Epilogue   173

About the Author   181

Preface

*S*tanding in his upright stance he placed his delicate, womanlike, manicured left hand on the bright green felt. As the wooden shaft of the stick moved slowly back and forth through his bridged left index finger, he stroked the cue ball into the rack. The balls cracked like an explosion—a bolt of lightning on a hot summer's night.

"I've been down on two ships.... been around the earth six times.... can beat anybody livin' for the cash. Jackie Gleason used to rack balls for me on Broadway. Times Square was my beat."

The audience loved it. Smiles and giggles were adrift and the air was full of magic.

Fats turned to the table, took aim on the three ball, and shot it smartly into the side pocket. The cue ball sucked back in a motion that defied logic as the crowd oohed and aahed. The cue ball ended up at the end of the table, lined up perfectly with the six ball for the next shot.

"I'm the best player that ever lived. Played every great player. They all got broke when they played me."

He chalked his stick and took aim on the six ball. So soft was the shot that it barely fell in, leaving an easy shot at the four ball across the table.

"I'm the world's greatest eater." He walked toward the red velvet armchair perched on a marble platform, picked up a freshly cooked turkey leg resting on the table, and devoured it in three bites.

"Most players get all nervous when they're shooting and lose five pounds. Me, I gain five pounds."

The crowd went crazy. Chalking the stick again, Fats went into his stalking waddle around the table and proceeded to run the rest of the solids. The last two were banked off the rail.

"I can outtalk any human from here

to Zanzibar. Won the world championship twice in Toronto, Canada. I can whistle in five languages.... knew every movie star, king, queen, politician, and maharaja known to man."

He shot hard at the eight, as if he really didn't care. The cue ball just barely missed. He looked up immediately and said, "Fooling with me is like messing with the plague."

The cue ball banked off the fourth rail and the eight ball at the same time, and the eight fell straight into the corner pocket.

Pandemonium struck as the crowd jumped to their feet, shouting and applauding. Fats finally broke into a grin, sauntered to his king's chair, and yelled "Rack 'em!"

--Personal recollection of the author

Introduction

There was something incredibly sad about the last years of Minnesota Fats.

The sadness didn't really have to do with aging, for if anyone remained "The Lion In Winter" until almost the very end, it was Fats, who used to dance his nights away in Nashville's Stockyard Restaurant or go on sales junkets with the author until just a couple of years before his death in early 1996.

The sadness had more to do with the way the last years of Fats' life symbolized the end of an era. Minnesota Fats came to Nashville, Tennessee, in 1984. His marriage of forty-three years had broken up; the IRS had taken him for something like eighty-six thousand dollars; he was in his seventies. It was almost as if he were looking for the last refuge on earth that could accommodate someone like him. If so, he found it for eight of the last twelve years of his life in Nashville's old Hermitage Hotel, and then finally in suburban Donelson, Tennessee, with his new wife, Teresa Bell Wanderone.

The Hermitage is a beaux-arts monstrosity that is beautiful mainly because it's such a contrast to what the rest of Nashville with its glass towers and neon downtown has become in the age of Music City.

The Hermitage is a relic of the early twentieth century, of the Women's Suffrage Movement—both the pros and antis used it as their headquarters—and of the Men's Quarter along Fifth Avenue with its saloons like the Southern Turf. It is a relic of the Age of Hustle in America at the turn of the twentieth century. It is fitting that Minnesota Fats, the man who epitomized the greatest game of hustle—pool—should wind up there. What is Nashville in the late twentieth century, after all, but the center of the biggest hustle of them all, the music industry? Some think life could have ended up a lot worse for Fats. He could have gone to Hollywood where he would have been fawned over and patronized and maybe become an extra in Columbo Movies of the Week. Or he could have gone to Las Vegas and become a greeter, like Joe Louis.

But his fate in Nashville was not completely dissimilar. The managers of the Hermitage were only too glad to have him on their premises. He brought a certain élan, a sense of danger or risk to the place, which was being renovated for the tourist trade. It was all a pose, of course. Minnesota Fats at seventy-one was hardly dangerous, and his hustle was largely relegated to his mouth.

He was content to spend his days on the sofas in the hotel lobby, chatting with visitors, stamping his autograph with his silver custom-made ink stamp. Sometimes he would pose for pictures beside the pool table the hotel put in the mezzanine. He might even shoot a few. More often, he would get a loaf of bread from the kitchen and amble across the street to the Legislative Plaza to feed the pigeons.

He was a harmless old man who had a lot of stories to tell. But he was also the last of the big-time hustlers, coming to a city that had become a Mecca for hustlers. When Fats died on January 18, 1996—one day before his eighty-third birthday—the reporters talked about the last of an era and conjured up images of Paul Newman and Jackie Gleason and black-and-white celluloid. The world, they seemed to say, was now safer and saner and a little less larger than life.

But the world had taken its toll on Minnesota Fats as well. The price of celebrity can be high. For Fats, it cost him his wife, money, and very largely his identity. For some of the other inhabitants of Music City, like Keith Whitley and Conway Twitty, it cost them their lives. Who says the world of the Hustle is any safer and saner than it was in the heyday of Minnesota Fats?

Some believe that Fats never quite "fit in" in Music City. He'd been through the town before, in the 1920s and 1930s when the Men's Quarter was still thriving, when the old Maxwell House Hotel and the real Hermitage were places of cigar smoke in back rooms, high-stake card games, and hooch hidden in a paper bag. Maybe that was the Nashville Fats thought he was returning to in 1984 when he left Illinois and drifted into town. What he found was Opryland USA, which meant mama and papa and the kids coming to hear music, and a kind of sanitized wholesomeness that would cause him to be looked at as a relic. So he tried to adapt. He kept a low profile, danced the night away, got old, and finally died.

That's one story. The other is that Nashville suited Fats just fine. It was a place where he could finally put away his mask, where he could wake up to feed his pigeons and tell his stories without actually proving anything. After all, there had been a certain kind of playacting to Fats' entire career. This was a man who spent a lifetime playing a tough guy in smoke-filled poolhalls all over America. But you know something? Fats never smoked. He never drank either. He never ordered anybody's legs broken. For most of his life he was happily married, had twenty-seven dogs, fourteen cats, and lived a suburban life in Middle America. During the last ten years of his life, Minnesota Fats wasn't even particularly fat. Maybe Nashville was a place where he could put down the hustle at last, at least a little bit.

Minnesota Fats was born Rudolph Wanderone, and he loved to tell stories. It was part of the hustle. A hustler can't hustle without the mouth or the confidence. But as Jack Dempsey once said, "It ain't bragging if you can do it." By the time Rudolph Wanderone became Minnesota Fats in the early 1960s, backing up his mouth had already become a lifelong obsession.

Fats was good, but how good was he? We know, for example, that in a series of televised confrontations with his old rival Willie Mosconi in the 1970s, Mosconi regularly cleaned his clock, even though Fats won the audience. We know that Mosconi once threatened to sue Fats because he kept telling the press that Mosconi had never beaten him for cash. Fats had a certain obsession with invincibility that only increased the sadness when, later, it became apparent that Fats wasn't invincible at all.

Fats was born in New York. If you didn't perceive this by watching the swagger, you knew it as soon as he opened his mouth. His voice was sharp and edgy and his diction was distinctly Big Apple: "Before we start running balls, I want to tell you a story. And this story is one that I would say has a moral—billiardwise, that is." When Fats spoke words like these, he sounded awkward, brash, and utterly confident.

When Rudolph Walter Wanderone was born in New York in 1913, he came into a world of brashness. New York was the "Big Banana," the Queen City, the place where the Gay Nineties became the twentieth century. It was the place where, in a single four-year period between 1910 and 1914, five million immigrants came through Ellis Island. That made it the true Melting Pot of the United States. It was also the place where, in the photographer Jacob Riis's words, "the other half" lived.

The first decade of the twentieth century was the beginning of one era and the end of another. Teddy Roosevelt went after the trusts; Standard Oil was broken up. In 1913, the income tax was introduced, as was the Federal Reserve System and the Department of Labor. In 1910, Mark Twain died and Halley's comet appeared—symbols, if anyone needed them, that the world was going to be different.

Into this world, in 1906, strode Rudolph Wanderone Sr., a Swiss citizen who had followed such trades as blacksmith, fireman, and plumbing and heating contractor. Rudolph Sr. was a huge man, standing six-feet-two and weighing nearly three hundred pounds. He was strong as a behemoth, once winning a bet by climbing on stage and lifting an elephant on his shoulders. On another occasion, he and several cronies won money by hitching their bodies to a railroad boxcar and pulling it several hundred feet.

Fats' mother, Rosa Bergin (or Burgin), was also Swiss, one of eighteen children. She had been married before, had two children, fled her husband, and came to the promised land where she met Rudolph Wanderone. She then had two more children, so Fats grew up in a family of three girls.

In his later years, Minnesota Fats liked to spin a curtain of mystery about himself and his family. Rudolph Wanderone Sr. claimed to have been a mercenary in the Russo-Japanese War of 1904–1905, and also claimed to have fought in several of the civil wars in Central and South America. Rudolph Wanderone Jr. told the same stories. Whether any of it was true didn't always matter. The point was to add to the image.

Rudolph Sr. did not worry about money. He believed it was more important to have a good time, and that's what he told his son. When his mother and sisters tried to enlist his aid around the house, Fats declined. His father took his side, saying "If you do not care to work, then you must not work, or you will be unhappy."

With one exception in the 1960s when he became a pitchman for a billiard table company, this was advice Fats followed all his life.

Fats claimed he began playing pool when he was four years old after a family pet goose ran into an amusement park pavilion and Fats followed it. What he saw being played in the pavilion was the game that has hooked generations of pool players around the world.

Pool is not a new game. It was probably invented by the Spanish and it was certainly on the American continent by 1710 when William Byrd of Virginia wrote in his famous diary that he had bought a table.

The game is more difficult than it looks and everyone thinks he or she can play. John Quincy Adams had a table in the White House; so did Harry Truman. But the game is a great leveler of social distinctions.

In literature and in history, a poolroom is a place of sin and corruption where innocence is lost. Many of the fictional adventures of George McDonald Fraser's Harry Flashman begin in poolrooms.

But our most enduring image of the game and its milieu come out of one motion picture, *The Hustler* (1961), with Jackie Gleason, Paul Newman, and George C. Scott. Fats, who was portrayed by Gleason in the movie, never had a bigger break in his life. The movie appeared in the early 1960s when American society was changing from the safe, dull world of Eisenhower's America to the drama, danger, and liberation of the Age of Aquarius. *The Hustler* was one of a handful of movies (*The Graduate*, five years later, was another one) that marked the transition. It helped stamp the image of the poolroom as a place where something bad could happen to you.

Some of the stereotypes may have been true, but in the immigrant's Lower East Side in the 1920s and 1930s, the poolroom was also a place of escape. It was a place where a smart guy on the make could walk away with a few hundred or a few thousand dollars and, more important, a name for himself. It was a place where the well-heeled could mix with the up-and-coming. The movie *The Hustler* may have ruined the image of the poolroom for all time. For much of Fats' life, the atmosphere of a poolroom was much closer to the following description from the early 1800s in Florida, when it really was a community spot.

> A billiard room is the general meeting place of everyone from the Governor to the laborer and the humblest clerk. Here, the shoemaker considers himself as good as the highest military officer. Here, in short, equality reigns. This billiard room takes up that part of the means of the inhabitants that is not required for subsistence. Here, one finds nei-

ther novelist or scholar. Here people play billiards, drink punch or other refreshments, and talk purely for the sake of talking. Here the treatment of travelers could not be more considerate.

In pre-television America, the poolroom often served the same purpose as the corner bar. More often than not, it *was* the corner bar.

Whatever Fats saw in that first poolroom in the pavilion stayed with him the rest of his life. There is no evidence that he ever even considered another line of "work." He was underage when he began playing pool—poolrooms in that period would not admit anyone not old enough to wear long pants. Because of his size, Fats was already wearing long pants, and it was not difficult for him to gain admittance to the poolrooms. Under the watchful eye of a friendly manager, he was soon learning the game. New York was filled with poolrooms, and he soon discovered one near his home in Washington Heights.

Fats wrote that he pulled his first hustle when he was six years old, beating an older kid out of a sack of gumdrops. Though he would later admit that he had lost matches, Minnesota Fats was adamant to the day he died that he was unbeatable when cash was on the line. After he reached the age of ten, cash was almost always on the line.

Fats always claimed that he had never worked for a living, but in fact he did. He worked at billiards. Saying that Fats didn't work at pool is like saying that Tiger Woods doesn't work at golf. Learning pool meant hours of practice every day; it meant closing his mouth and listening to and learning from the people who could teach him something. As brash as Fats could often get, he apparently knew when it paid to sit and watch.

His lessons came from a variety of sources. His family traveled to Switzerland several times to visit relatives, and it was in Europe that young Rudolph learned the intricacies of the game as well as some new variations: three-cushion billiards, where the ball must ricochet off at least three cushions before hitting the object ball, and Balkline, which requires that the opening shot be made from behind a line drawn parallel to one end of the table.

In Europe, in 1924, Fats' father had enough confidence in his son's ability to play the game to introduce him to Erich Hagenlocher, the German national billiards champion. Hagenlocher taught Fats how to play Balkline, and he laid the groundwork for Fats' mastery of a most difficult spin-off of billiards—one-pocket billiards, in which any eight balls must go into the same corner pocket. Fats always claimed, and observers agreed, that no one played this variation better. Fats was just eleven years old when he and his father came back from Europe, and if he truly was as good as he said he was, he must have been the Mozart of the poolroom—a child prodigy.

The written record of just how good he

was in the early twenties has not been preserved. We have Minnesota Fats' mouth and the testimony of a few friends who survived into old age. That's about it. Thus when Fats spun his tale of defeating a fifty-year-old champion pool shooter named Cowboy Weston when he was fourteen, you have to take it with a grain of salt. According to Fats, Cowboy was weather-beaten and old. According to Fats, "I really whacked him out cold."

Maybe. Maybe Fats was that good that young. Or maybe after sixty or eighty years, he wanted to remember himself as that good. One thing is clear: Minnesota Fats always gave the aura of being that good, which was almost as important. In the fever of the Jazz Age of the 1920s, when the confidence man and hustler had a chance to make a fortune not only in the poolroom, but on Wall Street as well, the aura of success mattered. The best way to achieve that aura was to go out and beat someone, anyone, in order to gain recognition. The local pool hustler would stake out territory and accept any challenge. He was the one who would protect the local turf and its reputation against the outsider. Thus when Coca-Cola, with sales suffering from the popularity of bathtub gin and other concoctions made more tantalizing because of Prohibition, undertook a nationwide promotional tour featuring "masked marvel" pool players, it was a big deal. Coke's players would invade the local hall and take on all comers. The locals would all crowd the building while their designated local champion took on the interloper. When Coke invaded Washington Heights, they got Fats. The prize in those days was a two-piece cue stick, and Fats won his share of them, enough so that he began to acquire an aura of invincibility.

Minnesota Fats was obviously a smart man. If you read or listen to his stories, you'll find an intelligent stream-of-consciousness style. His language was hard, unique, and distinctly American.

Yet it was American filtered through the experience of his European immigrant father. He could be provincial, but he was not parochial. His formal education ended with the eighth grade, but he continued learning for the rest of his life. The articles that were written about him as he aged show clearly how shrewd and inquisitive he was.

The Hustler helped Fats attain his most enduring nickname, and he traveled most of the world shooting pool, but it is impossible to think of him without thinking of New York. For most of his life he was, in fact, New York Fats, and it is still a name that seems more appropriate. His great rival Mosconi was the technical advisor on *The Hustler*, and he told the writers the Gleason character was based on a "well-known pool hustler named New York Fats."

There are half a dozen figures in American myth indelibly associated with New York in the Jazz Age: Mayor Jimmy Walker, Damon Runyon, F. Scott Fitzgerald, Grantland Rice, Babe Ruth, and Lou Gehrig. Minnesota, or New York, Fats should be among them. He, too, emblemizes the frenetic joys and pains of economic and physical growth, the crowds, the squalor, and the hustle of an entire nation on the make.

Fats was occasionally called Broadway Fats. From 1926 until almost the middle of the Great Depression, he made this part of New York his home, particularly places like The Palace Theater where he hobnobbed with such luminaries as Ralph Greenleaf and his wife, Princess Nai Tai Tai.

Greenleaf was, in Fats' words, the greatest tournament player who ever lived. And he had something that Fats desperately wanted: sophistication. He spoke well, dressed well, and had a beautiful wife. Years later Fats would call him his idol. Greenleaf, in a variation of Vaudeville, would perform intricate wing shots while the crowd at the Palace oohed and aahed and the Princess explained what he was doing. This was a combination of sports and theater—perfect for the 1920s and for the decades that followed.

Times Square was a pool hustler's paradise during the twenties. In addition to the Palace, Fats frequented Willie Hoppe's establishment, and Kreuter's, down the street, where the big shots of the game congregated.

Sometime during the twenties Fats met Alvin Thomas, a hustler from the Midwest who had changed his name to Titanic Thompson in 1912, just after the ocean liner of the same name had gone to the bottom. The two men were close friends for more than forty years, often running into each other at well-known billiard hot spots such as Norfolk, Virginia, during World War II. Thompson would bet on anything, from the number of watermelons in a farmer's truck to his score on the back nine of a golf course. He had long, lean hands, ideal for dealing cards and hitting a golf ball, but not, according to Fats, for shooting pool. Still, Thompson taught young Double Smart Fats invaluable lessons, not about the mechanics of the game, but the intangibles that went along with them: confidence in one's own abilities, and the innate ability to know what an opponent was going to do next. In short, Thompson taught Fats how to think.

Although Fats spent most of the period between 1926 and the mid-thirties in New York, he learned his greatest game, one-pocket billiards, in windswept Oklahoma City, where a hustler named Jack Hill spent six months tutoring him. In an age when the latest angle was sure to lead to success, Fats was no doubt surprised to learn that one-pocket billiards beat him back to New York. He had learned enough from Hill's teaching that he swept away all comers.

When the stock market crashed in October 1929, it meant the end of the good-time era of easy money and the New York poolhalls. The soup lines and bread lines stretched around Times Square; a lot of the fancy parlors closed. Though Fats never spoke of personal hardship during the Depression, the general economic gloom must have been a factor in his taking his show on the road. If the twenties had been the biggest collective hustle in the nation's history, the thirties reduced it to individual effort. Fats was a man who had boasted about never having held a job, and he was not one who had to worry about the factory closing, or the store declaring bankruptcy. He had already learned in his early twenties that the life of a hustler required living on the edge, all the time. So maybe he was better prepared for the Depression than most people were. Every time he picked up a pool cue, he was prepared to lose everything he owned.

From 1935 on, New York wasn't his New York anymore, and he spent more time away from it than in it. His life became an endless rotation: Philadelphia, Detroit, Newark, the South, the Midwest, and sometimes as far as California and back again. The Pool Hustler's Circuit became famous, as did the names of the players Fats encountered: Mosconi, Greenleaf, Irving Crane, Andrew Ponzi, James Evans, Marcel Camp. They made up a kind of roving brotherhood—rivals, but brothers in arms, men trying to hustle a living in desperate times.

Fats said the day he left New York he

was driving the most expensive Cadillac he could afford and wearing the best-tailored clothes available. As always, the image of the hustler was all-important. If you looked the part, you'd feel the part. If you felt the part, you'd be the part. Even before Madison Avenue invaded all of our lives, Fats understood that. Image was reality.

You had to know Double Smart, Triple Smart, New York, Chicago, Minnesota Fats pretty well to know just how much of the image was image. This was a man who could eat two whole chickens for a single meal, who constantly bragged about the "tomatoes"—women—who threw themselves at him, who played the role of the tough guy who was going to take your money no matter what. But between the lines of all the braggadocio are some telling images: Fats winning a farmer's watch in Oklahoma and returning it to him—he hated watches and having to deal with time, he said; Fats feeding starving compatriots in the midst of the Depression. Fats was the urban- dwelling poolhall hustler and womanizer who nevertheless stayed married to the same woman for forty-four years and spent most of that time not on Broadway or Fifth Avenue or even the Vegas strip but in the nondescript little town of Dowell, Illinois, near the Mississippi.

But the Mississippi was a place of legend, too, with its stories of Huck Finn and Tom Sawyer; the Duke and Dauphin, the ultimate hustlers; and the age of steamboat glory. The river in Mark Twain's world had always meant freedom. Maybe Dowell, Illinois, fit into the Minnesota Fats legend perfectly.

Evelyn Inez was the hostess and chief waitress at a watering hole in DuQuoin, Illinois, called the Evening Star. DuQuoin was a coal mining town in the heart of Little Egypt, which is what the hustlers called the strip of southern Illinois between Cairo and the hump of Kentucky. It was a land bounded on the west by the Mississippi River and on the south by the Ohio River—the two great rivers of American legend. Fats would drive down from Chicago, "clean out the locals," and enjoy the "tomatoes."

Until he met Evelyn. Night after night he returned to the Evening Star, and not just for the pool, the crap tables, and the poker. Most of all, he returned for Evelyn. It was a whirlwind courtship. The couple made one trip to New York for the funeral of Fats' sister and then were married in Cape Girardeau, Missouri, on May 7, 1941.

The couple spent most of World War II in Norfolk, home of the Atlantic Fleet and a very busy place during the conflict. It was a perfect place for a pool hustler. Fats was twenty-eight when the war broke out, but weighed nearly three hundred pounds. There was no way he had to serve Uncle Sam, so he did the next best thing—he entertained Uncle Sam's boys, and cleaned them out, too.

He wasn't the only one who lived this life. The hustlers and gamers who had to scramble during the Depression to stay afloat saw a new prosperity in war orders and the draft. Enough of them showed up so that Fats and Evelyn could rent a large suite in Calvert Park and host a series of Thanksgiving dinners for the old gang.

Making money out of the war effort was the ultimate hustle. The war brought a lot of things to Fats—Evelyn, money, and even more fame. The end of the war, however, marked the end of an era in American gamesmanship and hustle. It also marked the end of an American attitude that tolerated such hustle as strictly benign.

In the late 1940s the gambling industry came under the scrutiny of Congress. There were new regulations, and a lot of the old craps and billiard joints shut down. It was the beginning of an age of conformity. The Billiard Congress of America mandated that all tables had to be 4 $^1/_2$ x 9 feet in size, whereas in the old days they had ranged from 4 x 8 all the way to 5 x 10.

The boys had come home from the war and had no time for fun and games anymore. Hustlers like Fats seemed small-time after the United Nations had banded together to beat some real hustlers who had gambled everything on conquering the world.

Fats, of course, didn't like the changes. In the space of six years he was transformed from a high-rolling superstar of legendary status to a figure who seemed quaint and of another time. "A whole era had vanished," Fats wrote in his autobiography. "Big-time gambling was gone of this world, and it wouldn't ever be back."

So what did the Fat Man do? Well, he went home to his dogs and cats and turtles by the Big Muddy, the river of freedom and legend. He was thirty-four years old in 1947. More than half his life lay before him.

It is a fact that with regulation and the new conformity, it became harder and harder to find a game. Fats still went on the road out of necessity, and the money he won from cleaning out suckers fed him and Evelyn and the animals. But it was money earned at a price. The IRS would eventually catch up with him. The great hustler was now trying to hustle in a land that was just trying to get along.

Just how much money Fats earned in his lifetime has never been determined. At the time of his death, he owed the federal government more than eighty thousand dollars in back taxes. He must have won and spent several million dollars during his life, and yet it is clear that there was also something else driving Fats. As with all hustlers, it was the gamble, the chance, the risk that was irresistible.

After World War II the world began to close in on him, although Fats may not have realized it at first. The world he thrived in was a Hemingway-esque world of individuals and individualism where a man, for a while at least, could thumb his nose at society or respectability and get away with it. The huge All Around Masters Tournaments staged in Johnston City, Illinois, by Georgie and Paulie Jansco remained into the fifties. But after a few years and an IRS raid it just wasn't the same. The big money wasn't there any-more, for one thing. Without the lure of big money, shooting pool became a sanitized hustle.

The sixties and seventies—and a book and a movie—saved Fats from obscurity in a world now grown up and wanting to forget the foibles of the prewar era. Walter Tevis created a seamy world of vice and desperation in the novel *The Hustler*, and Robert Rossen turned it into black-and-white grittiness on the screen. Never mind that Paul Newman's Fast Eddy Felsen was too handsome for belief, or that he beat Jackie Gleason in the finale. Never mind that the real theme of *The Hustler* was redemption. To the baby boomers just entering college in the early sixties, it was supercharged cool. The same kids who lined up outside the college cinema to watch *The Maltese Falcon* and *Casablanca* and marvel at the anti-hero Bogart were wildly attracted to anybody who seemed to play the anti-hero role in real life. Now calling himself Minnesota Fats, this rotund middle-aged man who was happily married and loved cats and dogs found himself part of the great youth rebellion.

The officials at Indiana University in Bloomington, who hosted the National Intercollegiate Billiards Championship in 1962, must have known something was screwy when Fats showed up at the tournament, uninvited and unattended. His old rival, Mosconi, had been invited to shoot demonstrations, but this was supposed to be a sedate, serious event. When the judges and deans and professors got a look at Fats, they strongly objected. Why, we can't have this man on campus, they said. He's a character, a gambler, a hustler...

The kids, of course, loved it. They followed Fats around campus as if he were the Pied Piper and kept trying to set up a meeting for cash against Mosconi. For years afterwards, rumors spread that the two had locked themselves in the Student Union Building and had gone at it from 2:00 AM until dawn.

Another big asset to Fats during these years was television. He was tailor-made to be more than a TV actor—he became a TV character, guest-starring on the *Tonight Show*, *Wide World of Sports*, and eventually getting a regular gig on *Celebrity Billiards* where he showed such stars as Zsa Zsa Gabor the fine points of the game.

Nobody seemed to think of Fats anymore as that swaggering guy who hovered around the sleazy poolrooms cleaning out the suckers. There weren't very many sleazy poolrooms anymore, for one thing. The new places were roomy and air conditioned, with plush seating and waiters who brought you drinks. The game had definitely gone uptown. Minnesota Fats was no longer a man to fear. He was an old guy who reminded people of a riskier age. Everybody wanted a piece of Fats. He even got a regular job representing a pool table manufacturer and using the old gift of hustle to sell a product.

It's easy for a character like Fats to become a parody of himself. In the last fifteen years of his life, there is evidence that he did just that. It brought money to the table. But underneath the garrulous good nature, something else must have lurked, something of the old competitor, the man who went for the jugular when the money was on the line. The spirit often rebels against the aging of the body. Fats didn't want to get old. He partied; he went back on the road; he played exhibitions. He desperately wanted to capture what he had been, what the world had been. And somewhere along the line he lost Evelyn. The reasons are obscure, but anybody who knew Minnesota Fats can guess at them. He simply did not want to go gentle into that good night.

So he didn't. He came to Nashville instead, with its stars and music and with the Hermitage Hotel. Here he was able to act out his last scenes the way he wanted to—with bravado. He fed the pigeons and regaled reporters with stories of life on the road, of the legendary matches with Greenleaf and Evans and Mosconi. He married again—a woman less than half his age—in a chapel near Opryland. He danced at the Stockyard and Nashville Palace and rode in limousines. He kept the night at bay as long as he could and then he died, a legend.

The world finds a way to break all of us, Hemingway once wrote, and maybe the world broke Minnesota Fats. But legends don't die so easily. What you are about to read is a primer on life, love, and pool, by a man who came of age during a simpler, more raucous era, lived on the edge his entire life, and survived into the age of conformity. The Fat Man speaks.

8

Lessons From the Master: Minnesota Fats on Life, Love, and the Game of Billiards

Was He or Wasn't He

A lot of people question whether Minnesota Fats was as good as he always claimed. If there's any doubt about that, think about this: Fats hustled pool from 1917 through 1963 and never had a job, nor did he receive any outside money to support himself and Evelyn. In the trunk of his car he always carried between $200,000 and $300,000 in cash—crisp new bills—and two pockets were full of cash rolled with rubber bands. One roll contained larger bills for higher-stakes games; the other had small bills for smaller wagers. Neither roll got any smaller.

The Fine Art of Professionalism

Red Jones said he never saw Fats overload himself. He studied the opposition like a true student. His wife and traveling companion, Evelyn, said that before a big match the players negotiated the type of game and the amount of wager and handicap, if any, for hours and sometimes even days before the match was set. She marveled at Fats' success rate and knew that when the game was finally decided upon, she just had to sit back and count the money. Evelyn also said that Fats, in addition to his ability, was a great manager of his affairs. "He was very methodical and punctual. People always respect and fear an opponent who is very professional."

Never Beat a Sucker on an Empty Stomach

W.W. Woody took care of the old "could-Fats-really-play" question by telling the story of how Fats hustled a young collegiate champion named Nick Varner, who was later elected to the Hall of Fame. Nick's backer was Hubert Cokes, known as "Daddy Warbucks." Fats invited them to dinner, but Hubert said, "Listen, Fatty. We're not interested in eating, we came to play pool." "Why are you in such a hurry to go broke?" Fats asked. "I'm going to take you out and feed you. Then I'm going to bring you back here and bust you. No need to get in a rush about it."

Fats followed through with his plans by making fantastic three- and four-rail shots, all of which underscores Buddy Hall's maxims about Fatty: When he played for fun he was just plain good. When he played for cash he was awesome.

Easy Money

An old hustler's trick was for a right-hander to play left-handed in a strange poolroom and, after a few friendly games, offer to play opposite-handed with anyone who wanted to play for a little twenty-thirty. This was hustler's language for wanting to play for some serious money, and those players who played for big bucks understood the code right away.

Dancing to the Rhythm

Rhythm is the most important thing about the follow-through. Just like the player of golf or baseball, the pool player has to get into a consistent, natural groove. It's hard to teach, and it's usually in the follow-through where the natural talent shines. They've either got it or they don't.

Fats always said, "Finish your shot, Junior, stay down, enjoy it, and don't get in too big of a hurry to raise up and see your handiwork. It's like kissing your girl goodnight. Follow through and make it last. Finish the job."

The Eyes Have It

The rule is simple: If your vision is poor, don't play for money.

Puttin' on the Ritz

Fats always used to talk about being in stroke and falling into a patterned rhythm. When you're making shots, you'll notice that your comfort zone is increased. Your concentration level is supreme. The subconscious seems to take over. It's like that in any sport. Watch a basketball player when he's hitting every shot. He can't wait to get the ball. The same thing is true in pool. A wonderful aura comes over you as if you are infallible and the time between each shot falls into a pattern. More important, your opponent sees and feels your presence. He knows you're in a groove and his confidence is shaken. If he's smart, he's already visualizing the size of the bet on this game and trying to figure how much to bet on the next one. Usually it's less.

Attitude Begins with an "A"

Sooner or later you'll miss. Fats always kept calm after a miss. He was never afraid to miss. In fact, he often joked after a missed shot. Humor allows you to keep the confidence aura. This attitude sends a message to your opponent that you're not quite ready to take him out. Chalk your stick before you leave the table as if you're going to shoot again. As you walk away from the table while your opponent is shooting, walk proud, not slumped over or dejected. Love the game. Love the match. Be confident and happy. You are, beyond any shadow of a doubt, a fearless winner.

Amazing Grace

In 1965, *Esquire* magazine hired Fats
to write an article entitled "Proper
English: by Professor Minnesota Fats."
They dressed him up in a tuxedo, or
monkey suit, as Fats called it, and ran a
picture of him in the tux with the article.
When Fats' mother-in-law saw it, she said,
"Oh thank the Lord, Rudolf has joined
the church."

How Sweet the Sound

Of course, sometimes in pool, as in all sports, a little religion doesn't hurt.

"Sometimes you need a little religion when applying English," Fats would say. "The only way in the world you'll understand my kind of English is if you have a natural talent for pool. If you have it, you'll know after a while because the tough shots will come easier. If you don't have it, you'll never have it. You can teach some suckers the works and they can't sink the ball in an ocean. It's like the Cherry Singers from back in the olden days. They call them singers, which is all right except they couldn't sing. It's all the same thing with pool. If you can't master the table, you can't master the table. That's when you say a prayer."

Diamonds Are a Player's Best Friend

Fats used to tell the story of a great billiards champion named Robert Cannefax who devised and illustrated the Diamond System for calculating billiard table bank shots using three rails, and Fats claimed to have adapted the system for pool tables. The Diamond System is very complicated to teach. It involves numbering the diamonds around the rails and adding and subtracting those numbers to determine the outcome of the cue ball after it is banked off three rails. Fats said to go through the anguish of explaining it would be similar to the thrill of "watching paint dry."

No Way Out

Fats was a stickler for fundamentals. Over and over he told people to practice. A good routine he recommended was to set up an angle shot near a pocket and, as you make the ball, move the cue ball farther back from the object ball. Try pocketing the object ball by one of three methods: with a center ball stroke, with left English, and with right English. By such a process of elimination you will discover not only the proper way to stroke the cue ball but, more important, the proper speed to use in a given situation. Try this theory again, moving the object ball and cue ball all over the table. The possibilities are unlimited and the experience invaluable.

The Feel of the Game

In pool, instinct is hard to define in exact terms. You can call it what you want—feel, savvy, pool sense, the smarts of the noodle. But if you don't have it, you can play this game forever and never master it.

What Really Counts

No matter how he used to lecture on the mechanics of pool, Minnesota Fats always believed in the intangibles: practice, pool savvy, and, most of all, self-confidence. Believe in yourself because it helps you keep your nerve. That's the most important thing a pool player needs—nerve. You need it at the table when you've got to come up with the big shot. And you need it when the other fellow is off on a high run. Keep your head and wait until his luck runs out. It always will. Then you get up and shoot the lights out.

A Chip off the Old Block

Fats came by his reputation and accomplishments naturally. His father was born in Suhr, Switzerland, and was an adventurous young man who fought for hire all over the world as a soldier of fortune. Every time a conflict would break out, the whole family would get involved. Fats' father always insisted on getting paid in gold. It was risky to accept various currencies in those days and gold was good anywhere. Winning high-stakes games for money ran in the family.

Hanging His Hat at the Office

For a good part of the twentieth century, Lindy's was the most famous restaurant in the world. Lindy's was Fats' office; two flights up was the 51 Club in New York. His companions were people like Arnold Rothstein, Nick the Greek, Nicki Arnstein, Ed Sullivan, and Lou Walters—Barbara Walters' father. The Palace Theater, where 7th Avenue and Broadway cross, was pretty famous, too. For a young pool player, meeting the movie stars was an intoxicating experience. Think Fats was modest about any of this? Nope. "I've been every place on earth," he used to say. "There's no place I haven't been. I know more about geography than any living creature on earth."

Suitably Modest

Fats sincerely believed there were some things in the world he did better than anybody else:

"See, I go to a spot and tell them I'm a pool player and rob them playing cards. So I go to South America and play three-cushion billiards and beat anybody living. Cards? I beat anybody living doing anything with cards. I know more about cards than all the magicians on earth put together. I robbed every Greek and every magician that ever lived."

Rating the Stars

"The best movie star pool player was Gleason, and James Garner is very good. Fred Astaire was a player."

Looking the Part

"Every limo I ever had, I had suits to match the limos and shoes to match the limo. I was the best-dressed man. I had the finest tailors in the world. Only one man on earth that I would say could beat me dressing and that was Lawrence Welk, the greatest dresser the world has ever known, unbelievable dresser."

Stuck with Fats

"I'm playing this kid, who is one of the greatest players in the world, the 'Eufaula Kid.' Glenn Womack was his name, and I know all you got to do is walk in and they say, you want to play some twenty-thirty a game? When a guy says twenty-thirty a game, that means he can play. And that means you can play too, or otherwise you are an imbecile. So there was a little salesman, a fink out of this world, and he's trying to tell him who I am in the worst way. And he's scooting up to him and every time he would scoot, the guy had to move this way or that way. And he's trying, 'Don't you know who you are playing? Nobody on earth ever beats him.' And I'm trying to block him. I don't go to the bathroom for hours on end. I'm beating the kid and the kid's got some bookmaker and a guy that owns a bar across the street that's backing him, you know. So, to make a long story short, the guy finally got to him. And he says, 'Don't you know who you are playing?' He says, 'That's Fats. Beat anybody living.' The Kid says, 'I don't give a damn who he is, I'm stuck, ain't I?'"

Down the Floor and out the Door

"I played a guy, 'State Street Willie,' this is in the early thirties. You know that State Street is the 'hash' part of town. In the lower State Street, that's the skid row, where the Greek poolrooms are, and where the girlie shows are. Now this guy was a champion around there. He was a top-notch player. So, he came up to this other joint on the second floor and played me, and I'm playing him straight pool for fifteen thousand dollars. He's bringing in everybody, all the guys come out of their shoes. Guys come out of their shoes and socks—had money adhesive-taped to the bottom of their feet. So I broke everybody on this one game, and this shot came up and I had no shot at all, so I played a ball—banked it off one cushion into the stack and it kissed off the stack into the corner. I says, 'Three

ball in the corner.' They didn't even know
what I was going to do, you see? And I
split the pocket with it. State Street Willie
jumped out the window. And a cop
came up and said, 'Who threw him out
the window?' I told them he went out on
his own accord."

The Company He Keeps

"Know Dillinger? I didn't only know him, I was there, no further than from here to that wall, when he got hit—when they dropped him. See, what happened, I see him every day, this was unbelievable. But I was over on Lincoln Avenue. So, Dillinger, I seen him every day with black glasses. I used to say to myself, this guy is giving himself away. I mean, these were dark glasses, walking around looking in stores and everything. So, to make a long story short, I'm playing Willie Schram three-cushion billiards, one of the greatest players in the world. And this here, right on the corner of the alley where he was dropped, was a bar. I could see through the windows no bigger than that there, and when he dropped, the suckers was taking papers and napkins and dipping his blood for souvenirs."

Watching His Step

"I hustled craps at the George Washington Bridge, top of the bridge where they held the rowboats. And the little joint was like, not even as big as this room. And if you back up too much while you're shooting, you go right into the river, right off the top of the span."

Beating the Odds

"I'm the only guy in the world that would walk through Central Park three o'clock in the morning. The hoods would say 'That must be Fats; ain't no human that dumb.'"

8

Cleanliness Is Next to Godliness

"I don't drink and I don't smoke. I don't need anything to turn me on. I could drink that glass of iced tea there and my toes would stand straight up."

The Wisdom of the Ages

"In my business you better look behind you once in a while."

Using the Proper Ordnance

"A guy owed me some money and calls me on the phone and he couldn't pay me so he was going to set me up with Cannon Ball, who was this huge man who had solid gold teeth with diamonds in them. I tells this guy that I don't need to play him, I'll take him to my dentist—I'll have them teeth! The guy says, 'When can you be here?' I said I'll be there before you hang up. It was eight hundred miles to Houston. So I get to this fabulous joint called Reds, and I walks in and there's Cannon Ball. He says, 'I hear you been looking for me.' I says, 'That's right, Cannon Ball, but there's one thing you ought to know.' 'What's that?' he says. 'When I get done with you you'll be so small they won't call you Cannon Ball anymore, they'll call you BB.'"

How to Attract Women

"I drove Duesenbergs since I was ten years old. And I would drive after I played cards for four, five, six days and nights and then I'd get out, sometimes it would be like two or three in the morning, then I'm looking for the tomatoes. I was in the French Quarter of New Orleans. And as I'm driving slow here comes the most gorgeous creature ever lived and broad-jumped right into my Duesenberg touring car with the open top. And I said, 'Where you going, sweety,' and she said, 'I'm going with you.' She says, 'You got money?' I said, 'That's exactly right.' She says, 'I'm tired of those bums. I just picked up the tab for two or three bums in there a few minutes ago.' I said, 'You don't have to do nothing. If you know the magic words, you can be driving this Duesenberg tomorrow.'"

What Mobsters Do on Vacation

"Out in Phoenix I played in all the big joints. I'm in one of them and I'm hitting some balls and I'm talking and all of a sudden I see that something is going on. I see nothing but sheriffs and sheriffs and police and sheriffs. I don't say anything, you know, I don't know what's going on. I don't care. So a kid comes over to me and he says, 'Oh my God. There's two or three hit men in the joint, and the whole town is surrounded.' So while he's telling me this, another guy comes over and says, 'Fatty, them hit men is on vacation; they ain't working. They heard you was coming down. They was in Tucson, and they wanted to watch you shoot pool, you know.' I didn't know them or nothing."

Why Fats Never Got a Job

It was hereditary. Who can resist advice like this from your own father:

"Never do anything that makes you unhappy. An unhappy man will not live long, but if you're happy, then already you are a rich man. If a man has health and roof over his head and good food and good friends, what else does he need?"

But Was He Spoiled?

You bet. Fats had three sisters, he was the only boy in the family, and in his own words, they "worshipped" him.

"When I was two years old they used to plop me in the bed with a jillion satin pillows and spray me with exotic perfumes and lilac water."

The Robber from the Cradle

Fats began shooting pool when he was four years old, after chasing a family pet into an amusement park and seeing his first billiard tables. By six he was frequenting the Swiss Club in the Washington Heights neighborhood and hustling opponents. Fats later said he was ten years old when he first played for cash.

FRED WALTHER

Ahh, the Innocence of Childhood

"Every time a newspaper reporter
interviews me he'll say, 'Minnesota, where
did you grow up?' They all ask the same
questions and I always give them the
same answer. 'I was born growed up.'
And that's the way it was. I never was a
kid."

Ride 'Em Cowboy

Fats' first big match was against Cowboy Weston in 1926. Weston was fifty, Fats was thirteen. Here's how Fats described Weston:

"He looked exactly like the president when he's out campaigning. He had on a big white cowboy hat that was like, three feet wide, and he wore chaps and boots. Tom Mix and Hoot Gibson in their balmiest days never had anything to touch it. He was fabulous. When he finally got to the table and we were introduced I had to take a second look at the old Cowboy. He looked real glamorous in the parade, but up close he was all gray and weatherbeaten looking. He looked so old I figured he came over on the *Mayflower*. We played 125 points straight pool, which was all I knew back then outside of a little rotation, and once I got on the table it was brutal. I shot the old Cowboy clean off his horse and had the first notch on my gun. I mean, I really whacked him out cold."

Unmasking the Marvel

During the 1920s, Coca-Cola sponsored The Masked Marvel, a traveling pool hustler who earned a lot of publicity for his sponsor. The Masked Marvel was actually several people—and they all played against Fats. The prize for beating the Masked Marvel was a two-piece pool cue. "I won so many of them I had trouble giving them away," Fats later said.

How to Hustle a Hustler

When two hustlers hook up, it may take a long time to negotiate the game. During those negotiations, one hustler tries to have the up on the other at all times. For instance, if the first hustler wants to bet twenty dollars a game, the other hustler might say, "Let's make it thirty-five." Or one might want to play until midnight, while the other wants to play till one o'clock. It's all psychological, of course, and everyone wants the mental edge.

The Natural

"Lady Astor was the first woman to sit in the British Parliament. She was advised to take up golf for her health. She took lessons for six weeks without hitting the ball. She went out to the club and just watched her friends play. She studied stance and grip and swing, and she tried to develop each of these fundamental techniques herself before she so much as drove a ball. Now, when Lady Astor figured she was ready to start playing, she went out and toured the course in the low eighties. It was amazing. You know what that's like in billiards? It's like running fifty balls the first time on the table."

The Gift of Delusion

Fats learned early to pace himself.

"In those days I made my pocket money beating the suckers and mooches who came in looking for a mark and sometimes I'd play businessmen, like manufacturers and executives from the Garment District, or young songwriters or actors. I played way under my speed, know what I mean, and let them beat me a few. Then I'd really stick them up."

Better Than Fats?

Fats always maintained that Ralph Greenleaf was the greatest pool player the world has ever known. Greenleaf and his wife, Princess Nai Tai Tai, performed at the Palace Theater on Times Square, and the couple reportedly pulled down two thousand a week doing exhibition shooting before a packed house. The act, called Ralph Greenleaf, the Aristocrat of Billiards, Assisted by Princess Nai Tai Tai, consisted of Greenleaf, dressed in tuxedo, performing a multitude of trick shots while the Princess, decked out in a full-length ermine coat, strutted around the stage explaining the shots to the audience. To heighten the excitement, several mirrors were suspended from the ceiling above the table, giving the spectators views from different angles.

More Excitement, Please

Fats wasn't overly impressed with another pool hall near Times Square— Willie Hoppe's place at 51st and Broadway:

"It was packed with a hundred old men playing Balkline. It was unbelievable. The youngest kid in the place was like seventy, and none of them would bet you they were alive. It was like going to the library. It was like Sunday night prayer meeting with all those elders creeping around the table. Half of them didn't know the Spanish-American War was over. The only thing that appealed to me was the lunch counter."

Raising the Titanic

Titanic Thompson, who may or may not
have survived the sinking of the ocean
liner of the same name, was a pool hustler, card shark, and craps shooter who
probably influenced Fats' young life more
than anyone. He also gave an early example to Fats of how to make sure he won
his bets. Once when Titanic was passing
through Coffeyville, Kansas, he noticed a
large stone monument commemorating
the famous raid by the Dalton outlaw
gang in 1892. Titanic hired some local
folks to remove the stone to a feed mill
and have it weighed. A couple of years
later, he orchestrated a gathering of fellow
hustlers in Coffeyville and casually bet
that he could guess the weight of the
stone. To the disbelief of the others, Titanic
stated the exact weight and walked away
with several thousand dollars.

The Wages of Sin

On a visit to Oklahoma, Fats learned one-pocket pool, based on the premise that the player had to pocket eight balls in a single, pre-defined corner pocket. When he got back to New York, a gambler named Smart Henny set Fats up with a Coney Island shooter named, appropriately, Coney Island Al. The contest went on for hours and Fats whacked Al game after game. Most of the onlookers lost faith in Al quickly, but Smart Henny couldn't believe that Al wouldn't come back and win, especially after the handicap Fats had given. When the day was over, Fats had beaten all the bettors who had put money on Al, including Smart Henny, who told him, "Fat Boy, I've been betting propositions around pool halls all my life, but you cured me."

How About Just Plain Joe

Fats won his first nickname after defeating Coney Island Al. An onlooker wondered aloud that if Smart Henny was supposed to be the smartest man on Broadway, where did that leave Fats after his big victory? "It means that Fatty is twice as smart as Smart Henny," said another onlooker. Titanic Thompson then chimed in, "That's exactly right; he's twice as smart. Why, Fatty is double smart." For years afterwards, Fats was known along Broadway as Double Smart Fats. Fortunately, *The Hustler* changed his name.

8

Time After Time

"If there was one thing I never had a bit of use for, it was a watch. That's most of the suckers' problem, the watches and clocks. They become slaves to the timetables and they get a little behind in their schedule and they start running and running to try to catch up and they never do. It's a lifetime grief. I wouldn't give a quarter for the finest timepiece in the history of the world." Fats collected pocket watches he would win in matches, but was fast to exchange them for cash.

Breaking the Color Barrier

In the late 1920s, Fats and his friend, Hubert Cokes, also known as Daddy Warbucks, often visited the billiard room of James Evans, located in Harlem at 129th Street and Lennox. "Evans was the best Negro pool player who ever lived," Fats said later. "They wouldn't let him play on account of his color." It's an old story.

8

The Important Things in Life

Fats was hanging around Greenleaf's Pool Hall on Times Square when an old pool hustler named Willie Schmay walked in. Schmay, like many during the Depression, was down on his luck and hadn't eaten in three days. He had just begun a game when he fell to the floor unconscious. Fats quickly ordered food and fed it to the ill man. Within minutes, Schmay was back on his feet playing. When you've got billiards in your blood, all you have to do is refuel.

Check Your Thermostat

"All pool players play below their speed. That's the way it is. I never eat mashed potatoes with a hacksaw, and I never play my best if there's no cash up for grabs. If I'm playing for fun, I wouldn't care if Little Red Riding Hood beat me, but if it's a cash proposition, I'm like Genghis Khan going through the Great Wall of China."

Feelings

"It all boils down to the feel of a situation in order to know what you're doing when you stroke the ball. All the great players have it. I guess it's a sixth sense. If you have it, you'll know it; if you don't have it, try some other game, like tiddly-winks or ping pong. You'll never win a dime playing this game."

Fearless Fats

"I never knew any type of fear whatso-
ever in a tight situation and they all knew
it, the highrollers and the fun players,
too. That's why I couldn't get any serious
action once I cracked 'em all out. They all
knew I was absolutely fearless when the
cash was on the line and after they all
had a piece of me, none of 'em would
play me for a toothpick."

Ahh, the Good Old Days

"On the whole, the top pool players today are a lot like the suckers. They're scared to death to bet their own cash on their game. Oh, they'll tell you all about the tremendous pressure in those big tournaments, but they create their own pressure. What pressure is there playing all week long for trophies? Now when you're playing for the cash to pay the hotel bill and the food tab at the best restaurant in town, then I'd say you're really under pressure."

Man's Best Friend

"The best way to tell if a person has a deadly fear is watch them around animals. Animals are the most lovable and affectionate creatures on the face of the globe, even ferocious animals, providing they're not hungry. If a crocodile has just had lunch, he wouldn't bother a tourist in a hundred years. Only most people are afraid of crocodiles, even well-fed crocodiles. I never fear any kind of animal; in fact, I'm crazy about them."

Fats Goes to the Movies

"The movie was a tremendous flick, I mean swell entertainment. Everything was exactly the way it was, all except the last scene where Paul Newman beat Gleason for all the cash. That was fiction. I mean the worst kind of fiction, on account of I never lost a cash match in my whole life. But the most brutal part of all was the way Hollywood made pool players look like a pack of bums."

True Confessions

"Now, I was a hustler all right, only I never was a hustler in the bad sense of the word. I never hung out in small rooms near the bus station trying to beat the tourists and working men out of a quick deuce, and unless I was playing somebody in my class, I never tried to build up the other guy and make him feel like he was better than me so he would go for the whole wad. I always told 'em exactly who I was right off so they would know they were playing the best, and I never worked the sucker joints. I always walked in the biggest and best poolroom in town, the one where all the top sharks hung out, and I'd pick up a cue and say, 'Here I am boys, come on and get me.' And they all died trying. I mean really died trying, because I shot 'em down in cold blood. If you want to call that hustling, then I was a hustler because that's the way it was. I robbed 'em all."

A Few Tips, Please

Balance, Baby, Balance

Fats always said to grip the butt of the cue lightly about four inches behind the fulcrum point—the center of gravity. Balance is the secret. A finely balanced cue will have its fulcrum point sixteen to twenty inches from the butt end. Use your thumb and three fingers to grip— not the palm of your hand. The light grip is the right grip.

Practice

Nobody likes to practice their weak points. Fats knew that, and that's why he won.

Soft, Like a Baby's Behind

Fats never shot hard unless it was necessary. He always said your line is most important and you should concentrate on it throughout the shot, including the follow-through. Of course, too soft a shot will leave the ball short. Fatty always said you intuitively develop the right touch and feel as you practice.

Stick It to 'Em

Fats was an expert on pool equipment, particularly the stick. If he didn't have his custom stick with him, he would spend what seemed like hours choosing one. Fats always said he liked a twenty-ounce stick, and most of all, one that was straight.

Check for straightness by sighting down the stick like a rifle. Rolling it on the table to see if it wobbles isn't always a sure sign. Trust your eyesight.

Most of the cues used by adults today are 57 inches long and weigh between 15 and 22 ounces. The diameter of the shaft at the tip runs from 11 to 14 millimeters. Most well-made cues have shafts of hard straight-grain maple chosen for its warp-resistant characteristics. The butt sections are usually of a heavier wood, such as rosewood, ebony, walnut, or birdseye maple.

There are two general types of cue sticks: one-piece and jointed cues. Fats used to say that "all top-quality cues are jointed, but not all jointed cues are top quality."

Fats' stick was a Rambow made by the famous cue maker Herman Rambow. Fats always said he paid three dollars for it in the early 1920s and held on to it all of his life. Once it was stolen out of his car, but somehow through his contacts he was able to buy it back.

Jointed cues generally have fancier butt treatments than one-piece cues. Wrappings of nylon, leather, or Irish linen are often used, and the sticks frequently have intricate carvings and mother-of-pearl inlays. These various treatments aren't just for the eye; they give the player a better grip. Irish linen is the most popular wrap among the pros. It has the unique property of always feeling the same whether you're playing in the tropics or in the arctic.

A player shouldn't break with his custom-jointed cue. The shock will weaken the joint and ferrule and flatten the tip. Break with a house cue.

A Tip of the Hat

The tip of the cue stick is probably the most important piece of equipment a player has. Fats was a fanatic about his cue tips, making sure they were never worn out. Tips come in tan or blue leather. A good tip should be:

1. Properly crowned
2. Resilient yet firm
3. Slightly roughed
4. Well chalked

Imported tips, particularly French leather, are usually the best. They are chosen very carefully and are pressed by hand, one at a time. This ensures that each tip will have uniform texture and will hold its shape.

A Key to Character

Fats always said you can judge the quality of a player by the way he chalks his tip. But even good players can be careless about how they chalk the cue tip. Some of them go so heavy with the chalk you'd think they were drilling for oil. Others apply the chalk as an outlet for nervous energy. It gives them something to do with their hands. Most of the time this is a subconscious gesture. You've got to be careful about this, because the improper application of chalk can ruin your game.

How the Master Did It

Fats would chalk up after every single shot. He would apply several light strokes of chalk, making certain that it was spread lightly and evenly on the tip. This is the best insurance against miscues, especially when your game progresses to the point where you're able to use English—spin on the ball that changes its direction or speed when it strikes another ball or the rail. Chalk increases the friction between the leather tip and the slick surface of the cue ball.

"It's like a beautiful doll applying lipstick," Fats said. "If she applies too much, she's gonna look like a siren; if she applies too little, she might look like a ghost."

Standing Head and Shoulders above the Rest

Minnesota Fats' stance was different from that of most people because he stood almost erect, almost straight up. Fats said most people figured he stood that way because he had a fifty-two-inch waistline. But he always stood that way even when he was lighter and younger. He always stood erect because it felt comfortable.

Generally speaking, though, he always advised a player to stand about a foot from the table with the right foot in line with the cue ball. Face the direction of the shot with your head just over the cue in the line of aim. For right-handers, turn your left foot slightly to the right. Move your right foot back until the toe of the right foot is opposite the middle of the left foot. Be sure to distribute the weight evenly on both feet. The left arm should be extended, with the slightest bend at the elbow, straight to the bridge position. The proper stance, plus a little practice, can make the difference between a good pool player and a terrific one.

London Bridge Is Falling Down

Forming the bridge is one of the paramount techniques of pool. For the novices reading this, the bridge is the cylinder formed by the thumb and index finger through which the cue shaft slides.

The bridge must be short, firm, and closed, yet the shaft must have a little room to slide. Normally the distance between the tip of the cue and the bridge shouldn't exceed eight inches. Always use a little talcum powder on the bridge hand. The easier the shaft slides, the steadier you can keep your aim.

Different Bridges

Most players use the conventional tripod bridge because it provides firmness and thus good control. Some players, especially beginners and women, use the V bridge. The V bridge is formed by placing the palm of the hand on the table and sliding the cue over the fat part of the hand between the thumb and index finger. It is more difficult to control the cue from the V bridge. The tripod gives you much better control, but most of the leading players go to the V bridge if they have to reach for a long shot.

Back to the Basics

"If you have small hands or fingers, don't get discouraged, even though big-handed people have an advantage when it comes to making a bridge. Take heart from Joe Balsis, the 1965 Pocket Billiard World Champion. Joe's a champion who did not use the conventional tripod bridge because he had small fingers. So he had to adjust. What he did was place the last three fingers flat on the table and press the thumb against the middle finger. Then he formed the bridge by bending the index finger, letting it press against the middle finger with the end barely touching the thumb. It's not quite the same as a tripod. I might call it a fish-hook bridge, because of the way the index finger is bent. Joe called it an unorthodox bridge. It didn't matter what it was called, Balsis was an exception."

Getting out of a Tight Spot

If the cue ball is too close to a rail, rest the open hand on the rail, palm down, and slide the cue beneath the hand between the index and middle fingers. To ensure accurate aim, press the fingers snugly against the cue shaft.

Keeping Your Feet on the Ground

For shots that cannot be reached while keeping one foot on the floor, use the mechanical bridge. To be effective, it must be used accurately. Take your time and never be ashamed to use it. When placing it on the table, be careful not to disturb any of the balls. On occasion, you may have to hold the bridge in your normal shooting hand, because of the arrangement of the balls, and make your shot with the other hand. So what, as long as the ball goes in.

Switch Hitting

Fats always said it was important to learn to shoot both left- and right-handed. He said it would make "wrong-side table shots" easy and boost your confidence level. Don't fight learning to shoot opposite-handed. Once you do, you'll discover that your concentration level will be enhanced even further. Don't be ashamed to use the V bridge when learning to shoot opposite-handed. In fact, Fats recommended it.

Clean and Easy

The proper stroke is the culmination of the key fundamentals, like gripping the cue properly and executing a good sound bridge. Both must be consistent. It is worth long, hard practice because you can't shoot accurately with a tense, short, choppy stroke.

However, If You Must...

Aiming a pool shot is one of the most difficult things in sports, and it takes time. Don't let them rush you. First, take careful aim at the spot where you want to hit the ball. Then, as you take the warmup strokes, shift your vision from the cue ball to the object ball. Remember, you're aiming at two points, the cue ball and the object ball, and to pull off the shot you have to have good eyes, tremendous power of concentration, and lots of warmup strokes—tranquilizers.

After taking dead aim on the spot where you want to hit the ball, you go for the tranquilizer. Take as many warmup strokes as you need to be sure your aim is correct, check your stance and your bridge, then shift your vision to the object ball. The warmup stroke will steady your stroke, and as you shift your vision back and forth, the cue ball and object ball become trained in your line of sight. When you are confident of your aim and feel, shift your vision and your concentration to the object ball and shoot. Learning how to aim is easy—as long as you have the time to practice.

Looking for the Right Angle

Fats always said to take the time to study the angle or cut shots. The best insurance on an angle shot is to draw an imaginary line in your mind from the pocket to the object ball and to hit the object ball at the point where the imaginary line bisects the object ball. According to Fats, if you follow this theory, you'll drive the ball right into the pocket.

Splattering the Eggs

When Fats was on a run, he seemed to sneak up on the balls. He would always say, "Watch how you hit the balls. Don't whack 'em like you're trying to put them in orbit. Hit them real gentle, like they were babies." He claimed that 99 percent of the shots can be made with a soft, gentle stroke, like a surgeon's touch. Never wham-bam the balls. Hit them sure and soft, like you were handling eggs.

A Feel for the Game

You have to depend on your judgment as to how hard or soft your stroke needs to be. Sometimes you can hit the ball too hard and knock it out of line with the pocket or it might rattle in the pocket, whereas a softer shot would have gone in. Most shots miss because the stroke is too hard. When shooting hard you have a greater tendency to jerk or put unintentional English on the cue ball which causes it to curve slightly. It also puts a throw, slight English, on the object ball. This throw can cause the object ball to go off line by as much as 2 percent. Arnold Palmer always said his greatest lesson in golf was "hit it hard." It's a good thing Arnie never played pool for money.

Fats never shot hard unless it was necessary. He believed the line is most important and that you should concentrate on it throughout the shot, including the follow-through. Of course, too soft a shot will leave the object ball short. You will intuitively develop the right touch and feel as you practice. You'd better.

A Necessary Evil

One of Fats' constant reminders to his admirers was that English is very complicated and dangerous. When your cue stick strikes the cue ball anywhere other than the dead center, you're using English. Normal English is just a touch to right or left, up or down from the center of the cue ball; and the next degree would be called extreme English, which Fats said is "way-out English, like the far left or far right, or the bargain basement or the penthouse."

Striking the center of the ball causes no English on the ball. Use this shot whenever possible. It increases the odds of making a true, clean, and predictable shot. The outcome is purely mathematical and conforms to the laws of physics. The cue ball does what it is supposed to do after impact. It's not fancy, but you'll win more often by keeping it simple. Most

players don't realize that 80 percent of
the shots in pocket billiards can be made
without applying English to the cue ball.
You can be a good player without it, but
to become a great player, it's a necessary
evil.

And Furthermore...

Fats further divided English into two more classes: natural English and reverse English. Natural English, or high English, adds speed to the cue ball after it comes off a cushion or hits another ball. Sometimes this is called running English. It also widens the angle after it strikes a cushion and will throw the object ball to one side or the other from its original course. Of course, reverse English, or low English means just what it says. Reverse. It will have the opposite effect of natural English and will slow the speed of the cue ball after striking a cushion or another ball, which will narrow the angle.

The Proper Way to Spin

As a rule of thumb, Fats felt that the width of a cue's tip to the right, left, bottom, or top of the center spot on the cue ball is about as far as a beginner ought to go. "Don't force the spin on the ball," he would say. "Stay with your stroke."

Length Really Matters

Be careful if you decide to use English on a long shot, say, the length of the table. English will definitely influence the path of the cue ball to the object ball. You must allow for this influence. With English, that cue ball will curve as it approaches the object ball. It's good to know the effect of English on the path of the cue ball if you need to go around another ball that is partially blocking your shot.

Executing the Draw Shot

The draw, which is the backward, or reverse, movement of the cue ball after impact, is one of the few situations in which Fats would recommend using more than a cue tip's width of English, especially if you have to pull off a real "deep draw shot." To execute this shot, drop the cue down farther below center than you usually do for a light draw. You must also lower the butt of the cue so it will be as level with the tip as possible. When you feel comfortable with your stroke, snap your shot a little. This snap really puts the deeper draw on the shot. The farther the distance between the cue ball and the object ball, the less draw you will get.

Watching Out for Trouble

Fats reminded me that there's one more pitfall in draws. Usually you don't run into trouble if you can level your cue stick, but if you're shooting a draw when the cue ball is near a rail, or if you're forced to stroke over an object ball, that's something else. You compensate for the difficult angle by elevating the butt end of the cue in order to strike the ball low. If you stroke down on the cue ball—that is, if you hit below its horizontal axis—you will draw the ball.

Attending High Mass

There's one last form of English applied to the cue ball—the masse shot, which is French for maul. Fats was hesitant to talk much about this shot except that the stick was almost perpendicular to the table and you mauled the cue ball on the right or left edge. The cue ball would make exaggerated right- or left-hand turns on the table. It used to go around a ball or cluster of balls. There's only one problem: you can miscue and maul a table. Fats said it wasn't worth beginners tearing up a table. If you're ready to start thinking about a masse, you already have a Ph.D. in pool.

The Truth about Combinations

The most important thing to remember about combination shots is that they're in order only when a better shot is not available. A good thing about them is that they can be a way out when you're in trouble at the table. No matter how good a player is, the time will come when the only solution is the use of a combination.

Playing the Percentages

Fats constantly preached the importance of recognizing whether a combination shot was on or not. By on, he meant if the last ball in the combination was makable. If it wasn't on, Fats would say to look for another shot or, as a last resort, play a safety, a shot that leaves your opponent with a difficult shot. Fats used to get upset with pupils determined to pull off a combination that wasn't on. What usually happened was a bungled shot that spread the balls all over the table, setting up the opponent for a good run.

A Lesson in Terminology

When shooting combinations, you have to understand the throw of the balls. This is the same principle as the effect of English, in that left English will throw the object ball right and vice versa. On a combination shot, if the cue ball is hit left, the called (or object) ball is thrown right. Or if the cue ball is hit right, the object ball will be thrown left. For every action, there's an equal and opposite reaction. Ain't pool a simple game?

Two's Company, Three's a Crowd

It's wise to stay away from combinations with more than two balls. A two-ball combination is tough enough, and when the combination is spread out, it's almost impossible. Shoot them only as a last resort.

A Kiss Is Just a Kiss

A kiss shot is actually a carom, meaning the ball may kiss from one object ball to another. It's the opposite of a combination shot because on combinations you drive one ball into another to pocket a called ball. On a kiss shot, the object is to make the called ball carom off another ball. You may also use the cue ball to kiss off another ball to make the object ball. Sometimes the carom can be so light it's like kissing your wife on the run. That's where the name comes from. Of course, if you kiss your wife that lightly, she'll leave you.

A Sigh Is Just a Sigh

Kiss shots are frequently overlooked and are sometimes simpler than they look. Remember again that the closer the shot is together, the less green cloth you have to deal with and the greater the odds are of your making the shot.

Taking It to the Bank

Banks were Fats' best shots. He had a good teacher in Erich Hagenlocher, the German champion of the 1920s. This training probably more than any other single element allowed Fats to make a living hustling pool. Sooner or later any player is going to get tied up on a shot with nowhere to go. Whenever this happened to Fats, he could continue his run by banking the object ball. More often than not he would make the shot and continue his run.

How about Bernoulli's Principle?

Fats was no physicist, but even he knew a basic law of that science: The angle of incidence equals the angle of reflection. It ought to work perfectly every time, but it seldom does. Other factors enter into the equation, such as a hard or soft shot, or left or right English. A hard shot into the cushion narrows the angle of reflection while a soft shot widens the angle of reflection. High running English widens the angle and reverse English narrows the angle. Don't use any English at all, dead-center hit on every ball, and it's a fairly easy shot to pull off. Always remember that different tables have different rails. Their reactions are also different. Beware of the home table advantage.

The Secret is in the Planning.

Any Port in a Storm

The draw, follow, and stop ball shots are keys to position, but the rails can be a port in a storm when you want to move the cue ball into the proper spot for a subsequent shot. The speed of the stroke is the big thing. For example, a cue ball with high-running English applied is going to step up speed coming off a rail, so the amount of juice you give the cue ball will determine just how much speed the cue ball will gain. If you whack it too hard, you're going to roll too far, maybe three or four feet farther than desired. Some guys whack the ball so hard that it's liable to roll clean off the table and over to the lunch counter.

Speed Is Key

Running English will cause a ball hit off a rail to have an exaggerated angle when it leaves the cushion. So the speed of your stroke has to be adjusted for the desired difference. The big fact to keep in mind is that English works best on a soft stroke, so the softer the stroke, the wider the angle. But if you want to narrow the angle coming off the cushion, you would use reverse English. The speed of the stroke would remain the major factor. No matter what the shot, the speed of the stroke is always most important.

Taking Your Own Sweet Time

"Warming up is important. Some champions are so methodical they might take as many as a dozen warmups. Myself, I usually take two or three, sometimes four. That's all I need because I'm a fast thinker and very fast shooter. Some players just happen to need more warmups than others. Take Tuscaloosa Squirrelly. He would take fifteen before he strokes the ball. Squirrelly would shift his eyes from the cue ball to the object ball, back and forth, back and forth, dozens of times. And when he shifted his vision like that he would wrinkle his forehead up and down. It drove me crazy but it worked."

The Master in His Element: Minnesota Fats on Eight Ball

Know the House Rules

There are many variations of Eight Ball. Some players look to play bank or three-rail shots on the eight. Some play last pocket, where the object is to pocket the eight ball in the pocket where the last stripe or solid was made. Fats used to play a lot of two straights and a bank in which he banked every third ball, and the eight. Remember to check the rules on pocketing the eight ball on the break. In some places you simply re-rack; in others you either win or lose.

Piece of Cake

The easiest combinations to shoot are those where the balls are frozen together. Generally you can determine if the shot is dead-on if the last two balls in the set line up with the pocket. If they line up, they're dead-on and it's a piece of cake. It's funny how so many players overlook frozen combinations.

But Never More Than Two

Stay away from combinations with more than two balls. That's what Fatty used to say, anyway. A two-ball combination is tough enough, especially when the combination is far apart. When you get one, take a deep breath. It'll steady your hand.

Stealing Candy from a Baby

The easiest shot in pool is a short, straight-in shot. Pray for a shot like that in a crucial situation. Hit the cue ball in the center, unless you're playing for position on the following shot.

Hitting 'Em Where They Ain't

Position play is the heart and soul of billiards. Without position, you'll always look like a shoemaker on the table. Always leave yourself, not your opponent, a shot.

Is It Half Empty or Half Full?

Eight Ball is fifty percent ability and fifty percent knowledge. It's understandable to miss a shot or to lose a game because of your ability. But losing a game because of mental error or lack of knowledge is unacceptable.

8

Drinks Are on Me

Study your opponent, and handicap him according to his ability and drinking capacity. If you want to win, play sober.

A Level Playing Field

Check out the table before the first shot. Roll the balls slowly down each rail toward the pockets. Do they drift left or right? Are the rails lively, slow, or dead? Is the table cover fast or slow? Are the balls true, or are they chipped or cracked? Are the seams smooth where the slate fits together?

Sweating up a Storm

Sometimes it even pays to check out the humidity in the room. In a highly humid room, the English won't take as much, and the balls aren't as lively. Also check the temperature. A warm room causes the balls to be more lively.

NEVER BEHIND THE EIGHT BALL

The Bigger the Player, the Smaller the Table

If you are going to play someone who might be better than you, you will have a better chance of winning on a smaller table. The playing field is leveled when a good player plays on a smaller table. On the other hand, when a player plays on a large table, like a nine-footer, his skills become more of a factor and the average player will have a hard time winning. Years ago the tables in the South were smaller and Fats would sometimes lose there. But when he rematched on the big tables in the North, he would win his money back.

How to Break

The break should be head-on and dead center from the middle on the table, with high English, so that after impact the cue ball propels itself through the rest of the balls. You do not have to hit the ball like a wild man. Timing and a center high hit on the cue ball are most important. You can put a lot of speed on the cue ball without appearing to. Remember, the object is to scatter the balls all over the table for easier shots. When breaking head-on the chances of scratching are less than breaking from the side. A proper break is like a beautiful flower blooming.

Second Ball's the Charm

Some professionals say to break by hitting the second ball in the rack, aiming from the side rail and putting low English on the cue ball to keep it from scratching in the corner. This method is supposed to break the balls out even more, but the odds of scratching are greater.

The Brooklyn Rack

Beware of a loose rack, particularly when the outside balls are tight but the interior six balls are loose. This rack is called the Brooklyn rack. On the break, the balls fail to scatter. Most remain in a bunch near their original position and it is almost impossible to have a good chance of running the table. Always insist on a tight rack.

A Cool Customer

If you are a hothead or cannot keep cool, you will be a loser, guaranteed. Be cool or do not play pool. Showing no emotion can sometimes unnerve an opponent and cause him to miss. Fats recommended this strategy, but he seldom practiced a calm, cool approach. On the other hand, he was not a hothead and always avoided physical confrontations because he didn't want to risk hurting his hands. His hands were the tools of his trade. It was part of a game, knowing how far to go without going too far. Fats was loud and boisterous enough to rattle opponents and cause them to beat themselves.

It's a Really Nice Chess Match

When it's your turn to shoot after a break, study the positions of the balls and try to avoid those frozen in clusters or against a rail. The best balls to hit are those near the center of the table, or near pockets. As in a chess game, control of the center of the table is key. Study your potential runs, but do not always take the easiest shot on the table. Notice the position of the eight ball, and whether a stripe or a solid is nearer to it. You want to keep your work close between your last shot and the eight ball, so consideration should be given to the ball nearest the eight. Always think ahead.

Easy Does It

Shoot easy and, if you miss, your object ball will at least block the pocket or end up near the pocket. This could set you up for an easy shot and serve as a defensive move.

Offense Draws Crowds; Defense Wins Championships

There may be an occasion where you intentionally miss a shot to put your opponent in a jam where the opponent might have to break out a cluster, freeing one of your balls without a good chance of making one of his or her own. This is an example of defensive strategy. Sometimes it is OK to allow your opponent a false sense of security, but make sure it is false, or you will be the one with egg on your face.

The Shortest Distance between Two Objects

Always get position on your next shot. Concentrate on limiting the distance between the cue ball and the next object ball. Short shots are easier to make.

The Rope-a-Dope

Whenever possible after making your shot, try to carom the cue ball into your opponent's ball, knocking it closer to the rail for a more difficult shot. Try not to break up a cluster of your opponent's balls. Keep them tied up.

The Importance of Timing

On a long rail shot where the object ball is frozen on the rail but fairly close to the pocket, a beginning player should hit the rail and the object ball at the same time. An advanced player—particularly if the shot is long—should actually hit the rail slightly before the object ball.

Two for One

When an opponent's ball is blocking a pocket, you can sometimes try to make his ball and your ball at the same time by putting low English on the cue ball. This will put high English on the object ball and carry it forward after impact, knocking both balls into the pocket.

If It Walks Like a Duck

If you're playing with a superior player, it is best not to fool around with intentional misses, and if you have an easy shot, take it. Normally you would not be in a hurry to make a "duck," but an excellent player could keep you from getting another shot. Use "ducks" to get good position.

Remember, the Cue Is Key

Near the end of the game, always be aware of where you are going to leave the cue ball in case you miss a difficult shot. Leave your opponent a tough shot if you miss. You can always use the eight ball as a screen to guard your opponent from a decent shot. House rules vary, so establish whether the eight ball can be used in a combination or not. Normally the eight ball is not neutral. Hitting the eight first in kiss shots or combinations before you have cleared your balls is usually a foul, so it is wise to use it only as a defensive weapon.

The Longer the Better

When you and your opponent are both shooting at the eight ball, and you miss, leave him with a long, difficult shot if you can.

How a Famous Phrase Got Started, Maybe

Sometimes you get caught behind the eight ball. In a situation like this, use a bank shot, or shoot a masse shot to curve the cue ball around the eight.

One story about the term "behind the eight ball" says it started in 1919 because of a game called Kelly Pool. This was a rotation game where you shot the balls in numerical order. Before the game started, the players would shake a container containing fifteen little numbered pills. Each player would draw one numbered pill. This number would remain secret because players won who made the ball with their number on it. If you drew the number eight or greater, the chances of winning were less. So, behind the eight ball meant you were in a tough position.

What Does He Really Think?

"Pool is the greatest toy the world has ever known."

Epilogue

The day of the funeral dawned bright and sunny, but cold. It was eerie as we stood around Fats' casket at the gravesite. There was no conversation coming from Fats, no clatter of pool balls, no poolroom jargon or smoke-filled air, and no country music playing. Reality was beginning to set in—a piece of Americana would be no more. We were laying to rest Minnesota Fats, the tiger—ever-aggressive, always on the prowl, always in control. On the other hand, we would bury Rudolf Walter Wanderone Jr., who was a pussycat—calm, quiet, generous, a lover of children and animals, and a renowned humanitarian.

As the preacher delivered a few words over Fats' body, my mind searched for clarity about Fats and his mysterious and adventurous life. Why was Minnesota Fats so interesting? What was his fascination? He tickled our funny bone and tapped a fantasy in all that knew him, but what was it that intrigued us? Perhaps he drew that hidden maverick out of us that society, with its sense of what is proper, had suppressed within our hearts. Was it his air of complete confidence and boldness that stirred our passion and aroused our humor?

It was in 1964, during a television interview with Barbara Walters, that Minnesota Fats first caught my attention. When the several years of Fats vs. Willie Mosconi pool matches came along, my intrigue climbed to new heights. He was, to say the least, a nonconformist—one who went against the established ways and who gifted the baby boomers with a rebellious hero. He was a boisterous fat man who was hilarious and, at times, very skilled. If you ask ten people who won those matches with Mosconi, eight would tell you Fats did. Actually, Mosconi won them all, although Fats won some games within the sets.

Famous commentators like Howard Cosell, John Madden, and John McKay were enamored with the Fat Man, and television ratings for the Mosconi matches went "over the moon." America loved Minnesota Fats. He became not only an

American legend, but also an American icon.

As my mind continued to scan over thoughts and impressions of Fatty, it locked upon how we met. Both of us lived in southern Illinois, and Fatty was always playing exhibitions for college students or local charities. He often appeared on local television shows in St. Louis, and although he was not yet a personal friend, it seemed as though he was.

Little did I know that both of our lives would make a dramatic change in 1984. While a fresh new career awaited me in Nashville, Fats was ending his forty-four-year marriage and retiring to Nashville. What a surprise it was for me to see him perched in a plush sofa armchair in the lobby of the grand old palatial Hermitage Hotel in downtown Nashville. We talked and hit it off right away. Fats showed me a pool table on the mezzanine level, and then all of his memorabilia in his suite.

Over the next eleven years, Fats became a close friend. He told me count-

less stories—most with a lot of braggadocio, and some that seemed "on the
square," as Fats would say. It was the stories "on the square" that were marvelous
and mystic—stories that held me spell-
bound. They were stories that created an
insatiable desire to research and gather
facts to support or refute them.

After three years of intense research
covering the United States and world historical events from 1880 to the present, I
deduced that Fats had an incredible
memory and that many of his accounts
were, to a degree, accurate and quite possible. For instance, ship manifests prove
that he and his father traveled in 1924
through Europe, where he claimed they
met the Kaiser and Hitler. Interviews
with family members confirmed Fats'
father was a soldier of fortune who
worked for Russia in the Russo-Japanese
War, and who also worked for the Kaiser
in intelligence campaigns in South
America and Central America.

As the preacher wound up his sermon,
Fats' stories of shooting pool for large

stakes in the homes of Houston oil tycoons in 1963 came to mind, as did Fats' claim to have seen Dillinger shot, and of playing cards with the biggest gamblers in the country, and mixing with notables like Howard Hughes and Jane Russell, and hosting a multitude of Hollywood stars on his highly-rated television shows. It all answered my self-imposed questions as to why he was fascinating. Other flashbacks—of accounts of Fats beating Richie Florence out of twenty thousand dollars, and Las Vegas' Eddie Robin's historical data proving that Fats took down the world's best one-pocket player, Hayden Lingo, in 1948—all settled my mind to Fats' ability. He not only had the reputation, he also had the skill.

After the preacher finished, a female country singer performed "Amazing Grace." This really choked everybody up. Like an instant replay came remote visions of Fats feeding his stray cats and dogs; of Fats spreading bread crumbs on Legislative Plaza for the pigeons; of Fats giving thousands of dollars to out-of-work coal miners trying to relocate to Chicago; of Fats buying shoes and clothes for poor kids, and playing free exhibitions for charities, and always taking the time to talk to all the people. All of these visions seemed to put into perspective who Rudolf Walter Wanderone Jr. was.

The brief ceremony was over. Dignitaries chatted afterward, including the great world champion Buddy Hall, who let everyone know that "Minnesota Fats did more for pool than any other player in the history of the game."

What else could be said? The crowd dispersed and the sun was casting long shadows in the cool, crisp air when the crackling sound of a slow-moving vehicle on the gravel road nearby caught my attention. There in the corner of my eye was a big old weatherbeaten Ford LTD rolling slowly by the grave. Inside were two good ol' boys who appeared to be a couple of Fats' greatest fans. The driver hung his arm out of the window and down the door, holding a cue stick in his left hand. As the car passed the grave, he raised the stick in the air as a private goodbye to a fallen hero. Fats would have appreciated the gesture.

—Frederich H. Walther

About the Author

Fred Walther and his wife Margie were privileged to hear the fascinating stories told by pool great Minnesota Fats Wanderone over a period of fifteen years before Fats died in 1996. They visited their friend often in the lobby of Nashville's palatial old Hermitage Hotel where he lived.

Intrigued by the influences that helped shape Fats' colorful life and personality, Walther is now writing a historical novel about the Wanderone family. He has made several trips to Europe, gathering material which focuses on the life of Fats' soldier-of-fortune father.

In *Never Behind the Eight Ball*, Walther shares stories, viewpoints, and experiences related by Fats during those Nashville visits and during their travels together across the country in the early 1990s to promote auto auctions. In addition to biographical material, there are pithy observations about pool that are applicable to life situations in general.

Walther, who lives in Murfreesboro, Tennessee, is general manager of

Manheim's Tennessee Auto Auction there. The branch is a subsidiary of Cox Enterprises of Atlanta, one of the world's largest auction companies. Murfreesboro is also home to the Walthers' three children and their families – which include three grandchildren – and to Margie's brother's family of seven.

A dean's list graduate of Southern Illinois University in general business administration, Walther has been in the automobile business over a period of forty years. He has chosen to donate all royalties from this book to the Minnesota Fats foundation. The organization assists people who are in need due to financial or medical problems, and contributes to local humane societies. The nonprofit foundation was created to perpetuate Minnesota Fats' generosity to the needy. Anyone wishing to make donations to the foundation may send them to Marjorie A. Walther, 1538 Georgetown Lane, Murfreesboro, TN 37129.